THE SHEER GALL OF IT

THE SHEER GALL OF IT !

THE WIT OF GLASGOW

CARTOONS BY

WILLIE GALL

COMMENTARY BY

CLIFF HANLEY

MAINSTREAM
PUBLISHING

First published in Great Britain in 1988 by
MAINSTREAM PUBLISHING COMPANY (EDINBURGH) LTD
7 Albany Street, Edinburgh EH1 3UG

ISBN 1 85158 202 9 (cloth)
ISBN 1 85158 195 2 (paper)

British Library Cataloguing in Publication Data
Gall, Willie
    The sheer gall of it! : the wit of Glasgow.
    1. Scottish humorous cartoons – Collections.
    I. Title II. Hanley, Clifford, *1922-*
    741.5'9411

ISBN 1-85158-195-2

Typeset in 11 on 12 Plantin by Bookworm Typesetting, Edinburgh.
Printed in Great Britain by Richard Clay Ltd, Bungay, Suffolk.

CONTENTS

INDUSTRY

To be perfectly serious, and even solemn, the Industrial Revolution was one of the great forces in shaping Glasgow and the Glaswegians. What had started as a wee fishing village with a cathedral and a few weavers suddenly exploded into being the Second City of the Empire (though, as some irreverent keelies pointed out, it was also the First City of the Pavilion and the Theatre Royal).

It was an up-and-down affair, of course. Industries came and industries went. In the first half of this century, it all had a spurious atmosphere of permanence. Heavy industry was here to stay forever, the hammer's ding-dong was the Song of the Clyde and all that, and paddle-steamer passengers sailing down the Clyde got as much excitement out of waving to the riveters as they would get from seeing the magic waters of the Firth.

Beardmore's Forge was the centre of the industrial world. North British Locomotives, all that, and the rich sulphur-laden smoke that gave the tenements their proud patina and had generations coughing and spluttering proudly.

So nothing stays the same, and just as well, you may say. Factories and shipyards evaporated before our very eyes. But that is all a bit of the great Glasgow saga too. Without consciously analysing it, the common five-eight Glaswegian grew up knowing that slumps and catastrophes were always liable to be waiting round the next corner, and it was that certainty, or uncertainty, that shaped him, and her. We go through life braced for the next disaster, so that every disappointment is a delightful surprise. On the other hand, when slump strikes we can say "Ah telt ye", and feel quite smug.

In other words, the Glaswegian is the great survivor, and it's the endless see-saw of industrial history that has nurtured in him to a nearly unique degree the basic survival kit, which is, of course, the joke. See triumph, Jimmy? See disaster? Aw wan tae us because, like, we see them as essential components of the great cosmic comedy, innat.

So. Captains of industry may be concentrated on watching the financial pages to check how the share prices are moving, and calculating man-hour production figures and price competition. Hughie and Teenie see the operation as part of your actual rich kaleidoscope, and if it isn't actually a laugh a minute it's a good giggle every five.

How very irresponsible. How very subversive. The right-minded citizen cannot but condemn such reckless frivolity, and skip the next few pages.

"What's up wi' bein' a cowboy? Ronald Reagan wis a cowboy."

"Sorry, son, all flights are grounded until we get a just and
reasonable settlement."

"Ah thought they said it wis bein' taken ower as a Taverna."

"A' the best, son, ah hope yer work-in works oot."

"Sit-in! In these wans ah canny even sit doon!"

"Know whit the wife gave me fur ma breakfast when she fun' oot ah wis a Flyin' Picket? A dish o' watter an' a plate o' bird seed!"

"Ah'm even willin' tae take an unskilled job like yours."

"He's took the day aff tae rest fur the morra's strike."

"It's no' often ye get a show all comedians an' nae singers."

"Whit are we makin the day, Wullie, Escorts, Austin Maestros or B.M.W.s?"

"I should be so lucky."

"Ah suggest we put a warnin' on every packet sayin' that failin' tae smoke more cigarettes could result in 1000 redundancies in Glasgow an' Stirling."

"This is wan thing we can whack the Japs at, Wullie ... runnin' joab centres."

"If Wullie wis Ian MacGregor he widnae close any pits, sure ye widnae, Wullie?"

"Ma take hame pay's only fifty quid by the time ah get hame."

"Campbeltown Loch I wish you were petrol, Campbeltown Loch, ooch aye —"

"An' remember, wance ah'm on the Board o' Directors doon at the works, you pack in the bingo an' play bridge an' go roon' wi' Meals-On-Wheels instead o' roon' tae the bookies'."

"At least, Wullie, sunrisin'll make a change fae moonlightin'."

"An' don't keep sayin, 'Pardon'."

"Wur latest idea is tae come oot oan strike first an' decide whit fur efter."

"As wan civil servant tae anither, if you get ma plane away tae Majorca on time ah'll forget aboot your income tax."

"So that you can enjoy the office party as usual, Jackson, we've decided not to tell you you're redundant until after Christmas."

"They say there's a good livin' fiddlin' the Social Security."

"This work sharin's a rerr idea as long as somebody else is daein' ma share."

"Huv ye decided yet whit ye're daein' aboot the T.U.C. Day of Action on Wednesday?"

"If ye don't hurry up ye'll be late fur yer go-slow."

SHOPPING

Where are ye gaun, ma bonnie wee lass, where are ye gaun, ma dearie? Where are ye gaun, ma bonnie wee lass? A message for ma mammy.

We are going to cry this section Shopping, but the Scots do not actually go in for shopping . They go messages. To other races, out there beyond the pale, a message means something quite other – a piece of information. To the Scot, a message is a half-pound of margarine or a fourpit of flour. Stand up anybody who can define a fourpit of flour.

And when I went the messages on a Saturday, at Andrew Cochrane's in Shettleston Road, they always included a two-pound pot of rhubarb-and-ginger jam. What in the name of God has happened to rhubarb-and-ginger jam? All things pass away, but I mourn that passing in particular.

All right, a fourpit of flour is half of a quarter-stone, one-and-three-quarter pounds. Hands up all those who got it right.

Okay, let's wallow in nostalgia for another minute or two. Another message in those far-off days was thruppence-worth of vegetables for soup. I now suspect, in retrospect, that Tam Cole, the manager of Andrew Cochrane's, had that concession to himself. He had some wee dutiful fink who cycled to the fruit market to get cheap turnips and carrots and so on, and Big Tam made a fortune from selling bundles of the stuff at thruppence a shot – they lasted us for a week. Nowadays, he would run an oil-rig on the side. But it keeps changing, doesn't it? Grown men are now known to go the messages. They do it in their motors and they do it in supermarkets.

Not everything has changed in Glasgow. I myself do go the messages, quite shamelessly, though it is or was well known that only cissies would do such a thing. In my early days in the newspaper business I used to share a late shift with another teenager, and I would cheerfully nip out for fish suppers for us. When it got to his turn he flatly refused, so I got one fish supper and ate it in front of him, and to hell, he could starve.

When we first acquired a charwoman, christened Bodie by the weans because they were too young to pronounce Maloney, the dear lady was absolutely staggered to see me wheeling the pram down the street to buy a pint of milk. Your macho Glesca husband would have died rather than do either. Shopping? Women's work.

It went farther. When I was young and daft, and devoted to amateur carpentry, I used to buy tools from a second-hand shop in the Saltmarket. I swear to you that one Saturday morning I found a married couple staring at the window, the husband picking his selection, and then the wife going in to buy the planes or saws or whatever, because no masculine male would be seen dead in a shop.

More, more! In the days of custom-built suits, I have seen a similar couple staring into a window of the Fifty-Shilling Tailors in Argyle Street, the wife going in, and bringing out a chap with a measuring tape and sizing up the man on the pavement, to save him the horror of entering the store.

And to this very day, if you wander through the car park of a supermarket, you will see parked cars containing a husband who on being sighted will whisk a *Daily Record* in front of his face to guarantee his anonymity. Okay for the wife to go in there and wheel the trolley, but it would not be seemly for a human adult male to be connected with such a jessified activity. Even if the trolley wheels are dodgy and she has to put the thing on her wee shoulders to get it to the boot, that is woman's work.

All right, things do change. Hughie will sometimes force himself to accompany Deirdre to the stores, and even furtively mutter that he would rather have Edam than cheddar. But it is a very weird ritual, shopping in Scotland. It still separates the men from the pansies.

And it is all a great lottery. You make a dive for that checkout with only one wummin in front of you, and as you line up, somebody shoves up a notice saying CHECKOUT CLOSED.

Oh, it's all high-tech and Gulliverised. And some of the patter is very good too. I suppose it's just senility that turns my mind to the magic days of Andrew Cochrane's and tuppence-worth of vegetables for soup. On the other hand, the lassies who work in shops are just as cheeky as ever, and the customers are still flaming nuisances.

So nothing changes, really. Innat no nice?

"Ah hope an' trust ye'll never sell oot tae wan o' thae big American conglomorates, Mrs Montgomery."

"Ah'll take hauf a pun o' thae Israeli links Strathclyde's goin' oan aboot."

"Ah think we're on camera two, Mrs Wilson."

"If Shylock knew how much a pound o' flesh costs nowadays he'd turn in his grave."

"Listen, hen, ah can remember when gas only went up if ye put a match tae it."

"Ah see youse butchers is huvin' a bad time, Jimmy, but ah bet the coos is delighted."

"Something that won't detract from his insignificance."

"One bottle of this sun-tan lotion, madame, and you'll require the protection of the Race Relations Board."

"I wish to see the latest in antiques."

"Actually, we're a multinational, ah'm Scotch, the wife's English an' the dug's an Alsatian."

"When are ye gettin' yer frozen prices in?"

'Of course, you must remember, madame, mahogany doesn't grow on trees."

"Ah want her measured fur a bottle o' sun-tan lotion!"

"Is it true ye're oan the United Nations blacklist because ye only sell white puddin's, Jimmy?"

"How iss it, Angus, that you have the old fashioned pumps but not the old fashioned prices?"

"Ah don't think ah'd suit that colour, Agnes!"

"When ma man heard that white's the fashion this summer he bought me a bottle o' bleach."

"A perr o' boxer shorts, light welterweight."

"Naw, ah don't want tae sniff it, it's tae mend ma kitchen chair."

"These are fae Tai Wan, try wan."

"It's a terrible joab decidin' whit tae panic buy next, i'ntit?"

"O.K., it's no' very big ... whit dae ye expect fur five quid, Notts Forest?"

"Huv ye a nice big, long football player?"

"Could ye come an' take oot yer double glazin' noo the winter's ower!"

"Actually, under the counter for special customers we huv beefburgers, chips an' big cream cakes."

"Say, for instance, Charles calls the whole thing off!"

"Ah suppose ah'd better send wan tae ma man as well."

"Ah'd be feart tae put it oan in case ah got anither man."

"Ye've a sin tae answer for, sellin' me a' thae fags!"

"Business is terrible, even the fast food's slow."

"An' remember, ye're no' tae waste the firm's time by smilin' tae customers."

"Things that's in short supply always seem tae be scarce!"

"I would point out, my friend, that you're no' cheaper than the guy up the road, it's jist that he's dearer."

"Ah've been that busy shoppin' around ah've went an' forgot whit ah came oot fur."

"Huv yiz any short long johns?"

'If there's wan thing ah can't stand, Michelle, it's customers that come in wantin' tae buy things."

"How much is yer tuppeny pies this week that wis ninepence last week?"

"The boss is aff no' weel."

"Seein' it's Shrove Tuesday, toss a couple o' thae pancakes intae a poke fur me, hen."

"Haw, Debbie-Jane, fetch the steps, this yin wants high fibre."

"A wee cheap one, it's jist for somebody wi' a sair heid."

POLITICS

Scotland probably *invented* politics. I mean, sex is secondary to a good argy-bargy. Some might say that sex itself is only an argy-bargy, but such people are only looking for an argy-bargy.

If we can skip lightly over religion (and in Scotland you need a pole-vaulter's stick to skip lightly over religion) dear old John Knox had something to do with it, because he was into everything argumentative, including a teenage lassie whom he married when he looked like a done old man. Like, he disapproved of sex except when it was available to him.

Everything in this crazy country, and certainly in this crazy city, turns into a big philosophical dispute. Has anybody any recollection today of the materialist conception of history? Whit? In the old ILP the comrades called it the MCH, just to confuse any M15 agents who might be bugging the wee hall in Bridgeton. It had something to do with Marx, I seem to remember, and I was a devoted fan of the Marx Brothers, even including Karl, though the boys had dropped him from the act by then because he couldn't play the harp very well.

In that golden age, when life was fairly hellish, but when your actual Glasgow leftie knew that, come the revolution, the world would be pure heaven by next Tuesday at 3.30 p.m., life was already pure heaven because the left-wing keelie lived with the conviction of The Ideal.

There were many times, maybe after a dance, or a meeting at Cranston's, when three or four of the enthusiasts would stroll quietly home, to where one of them lived, and say goodnight, and then the home body would rejoin the gang to walk the second member home, and the second one would decide to keep walking to make sure the third eejit got home, because there was still so much to talk about. I mean, the universe had to be sorted out that very night, and no' the morra.

But what about the antisissygy? I mean, the essential oppositeness of everything. I have looked that word up in five dictionaries, and it isn't there. I got it from Hugh MacDiarmid,

via Iain Cuthbertson, and maybe they invented it. Scots invented everything, and maybe they go in for inventing words when they can't think up a steam engine.

Where was I? I will tell you, in politics in Scotland it is not easy to remember where you were. We were talking about the antisissygy, or something. Well, it's the separation kind of thing – the gap between the ideal and what actually happens, and what actually happens is Toon Cooncillors, who are more devoted to their expenses than to the liberation of man, or women, or collie dugs, or whatever.

So the Scots are passionately political, when it comes up their humph, and then, as soon as they have voted for their favourite candidate, they realise that politicians of any colour are a load of rubbish. So why do they keep voting for them? Easy. Because it's easier to vote than to be a member of that load of rubbish. Let the illiterate bums get on with it.

This is an awful story I am about to tell, but I have no mercy. When I was writing a story about Dundee some years ago, I organised a wee lunch where I could meet some of the important people and get a sort of road-map from them. At the time, I think the Lord Provost and several councillors were in the nick for over-enthusiasm or something. Well, one of my guests, a town councillor, felt impelled to tell me that although the town's industries were in a bad way, the tourist industry was flourishing, with weekly plane-loads from Sicily full of chaps who were coming for refresher courses.

So we in Scotland are reasonably cynical about politics. To our superiors in England, we look like wild Lefties determined to bring down the British Empire, and a bit late about it. To ourselves, we are the advanced race who have realised that politics is a daft wee game played by people who couldn't qualify as moshie champions and who therefore feel a bit downput. Sad, really. They are downput. We put up with them by the simple Glesca trick of pretending they're not there. And in this situation, Glasgow is not entirely daft. If you can pretend for long enough that politics isn't there, maybe it will go away.

It will not go away, of course. But it can be contained by sniggering at it. Feel free to snigger.

"Ye never know where ye are, sure ye don't, wi' this bank
rate jumpin' up an' doon."

"If a young fella ca'd Mark Thatcher ever comes tae the door floggin' ile wells, bags o' cement or racin' caurs hunt him fur his life."

"Of course, the fact that you know every pub on the Costa Brava like the back of your hand doesn't necessarily mean that you are a suitable candidate for a seat in the European Parliament."

"Ay'm dyin' tae buy mine. There's nuthin' ah like better than damp runnin' doon the walls an' a bunged up sink."

"Whit ah'll miss is a' thur pamphlets for lightin' the fire."

"If there's no' goin' tae be a wage freeze why is the safe bein' replaced by a fridge?"

"For these are my mountains!"

"Awfu' unsettlin', i'ntit? Ye don't know whether tae start yer spring cleanin', book yer holidays, wash yer herr nor nuthin'."

"Are we needin' ony canvas, Andra?"

"Ah tell ye this — ye widnae catch me goin' oan a state visit tae Japan!"

"Now ah suppose the price o' battleships'll go up!"

"Would you mind terribly, Fiona, if I voted in favour of Civil Disobedience?"

"Don't panic if ye hear a bang, Jimmy, it'll jist be anither works shuttin' doon."

"Ah widnae go an play fitba' in Chile, wid you Gladys?"

"That, ah take it, covers the whole bloomin' lot."

"O.K., Jimmy, where d'ye want tae start, the front green or the back green?"

"Your candidate, Ladies and Gentlemen, has had vas European experience, having travelled extensively Loret Del Mar, Torremolinos and Benidorm."

"Are they floggin' the biggest Gas Showroom o' the lot ... Westminster?"

"Rerr weather fur slingin' mud!"

"Never mind whit ye'll dae tae Galtieri ... whit aboot the new dustbin lids ye promised us last time ye got in?"

"Kiddin' oan he canny afford a jaicket, ah expect."

"Tae devolute, tae break away an' rule yersel is fine. Ah hope it works when there's nae oil tae be your Valentine."

"Listen son, ah remember Shirley Williams when she wis wee lassie in ringlets singin' 'Animal Crackers in M Soup'."

"Which jist goes tae show they're no' as daft as we thought."

"Ah propose we twin wi' two ither towns an' then we'll be triplets."

"Big smasher that Paddy Ashdown. Wish ah could remember the name o' his party."

"See that Heath!! If it hadnae been fur damagin' the cocktail cabinet ah wid huv drove wan o' wur caurs straight through the colour telly!!"

"Fantastic? Us workin' class should be imancipated by the end o' the week."

"If that lot wis staged over fifteen rounds in the Kelvin Hall they wid draw a bigger crowd than Jim Watt."

"It's jist like bein' mairrit — ye canny win but ye canny get oot."

"Jist making out my list of New Year devolutions, dear."

"Whit's this then, Wullie? A conference or a flamin' flower show?"

"Nice tae know they'll be deliberate."

"I'm from the Monopolies Commission."

"Whit wi' deflatin' an reflatin' ye wonder whether it's an economy we're runnin' or jist a big balloon."

"Ah wish Maggie wid make up her mind, ma apathy's gettin oot of control."

"An' the first comedian that says we need sweepin' changes gets flung oot."

"Whit's a' this aboot Tory wets? Ah thought a' Tories wis wet."

"Haw, Kevin, dae you get the impression there's goin' tae be a June election."

"Basically, ah demand an on-goin' comparability dialogue situation at grass-roots level in respect of a responsible, copper bottomed bargaining structure at this point in time an' that."

"It's left tae me tae say it's only right tae advise Neil tae move left fae the right before there's nae right left."

"If we could jist prove, comrades, that she's a half-cousin o' Kurt Waldheim we'd be home an' dry."

"Well, whit party are you canvassin' fur?"

"Trouble is ah don't know whether tae buy a double or a single decker."

"Nae sign o' metal fatigue therr, Wullie."

"Terrible worry, i'ntit, wonderin' whether the election's tae be on the 3rd or 10th October."

"Ah don't fancy gettin' devolved at ma time o' life, dae you, Agnes?"

"See this Poll Tax, don't tell me we'll huv tae pay the full rate on him."

"Ah wonder if she realises she widnae jist be gettin' a husband she wid be gettin' a mother-in-law."

"That'll be the greatest tooth paste commercial of all time."

"There must be easier ways tae escape than that!"

"Ah fancied a wee change, did you no'?"

"Aw come on, Jimmy, it's no' ferr ca'in the council meetin' a fiddlers rally."

"Of course, if there's nae strike ah'll expect ye tae take it a' back."

"Ah hope somebody telt them tae switch aff first."

"Ratecapping, my dear, is like handicapping, only worse."

"That'll be in case they give ye a wrong number."

SPORT

People have been kicking and throwing things about since the human race got down off the trees, and maybe even earlier. So nobody really knows where exactly our modern sports began, though we do know a lot of them end up in the boozer for non-action replays of the day's game.

There is a fairly flimsy theory that the Scots originated football as the fairly crude pastime of kicking Roman helmets about, sometimes with the heads still inside them. Well, it's not too flimsy a theory, maybe.

There is some argument about where golf came from. The Belgians in early times knocked things about with sticks, anything from small stones to nagging women. Foreigners are always trying to horn in on our innovations. It does seem clear that it was a Scotsman, a sadist of some kind, who introduced the hole in the ground, to drive future generations insane with disappointment. But the wild generosity of the Scots is shown by their willingness to share the thing with lesser breeds outwith the law, although it must have been perfectly obvious that a lot of unfeeling foreigners would knock hell out of us at the grand old game.

The export of golf was of course a fiendish form of sadism. If muffed three-inch putts were driving us mad with grief, we just made sure other people would get suicidal too. We can survive it, of course, because we are stoic pessimists, we live in hourly expectation of the worst, so that every disappointment is a delightful surprise. Many foreigners are optimists, so that life is a recurring hell for them, and golf is one of the red-hot furnaces, ha ha ha.

As a by-product, of course, golf has generated more jokes than any other activity barring sex and religion, and they sometimes blend, as in the case of the man who postponed the critical putt of the match to doff his cap and stand to attention as a funeral cortège passed the road hole. To his opponent, staggered at such courtesy in a moment of crisis, he pointed out

that it wasn't every day his wife got buried.

And there is the curious tale of heavenly golf, in which Peter, Michael and Gabriel enlisted Jesus to make up a foursome. He played last and duffed it a few yards, but before it stopped a rabbit popped out of a hole, stole it and bounded down the fairway, only to be swooped on and carried skywards by an eagle; whereupon it dropped the ball and the ball bounced merrily along to drop into the first hole. Michael raised a hand. "Now, before we go any further, are we playing golf or messing about?"

Golfers of little faith will nevertheless pray, or curse, and those who are tempted to underestimate how many swipes they made to get out of the rough must be secretly aware that every one was noted by the Big Handicapper in the Sky.

There is a report, surely authentic, of a Wee Free minister on a solo golfing holiday who had six days of relentless sleet till the sun shone bright and clear on the sabbath, and being in civvies, he yielded to temptation and went out to try the course. This was noted by an archangel and reported to God, who immediately created a hole-in-one for the sinner.

"That's a punishment?" asked Gabriel.

"Whom can he tell?"

And the ultimate demonstration of unpopularity is the player who phoned an acquaintance to suggest a game on Saturday, to be told, "Sorry, we've already made up a three."

The peculiarly Scottish thing about golf is that it is the ball game in which you don't play against an opponent. You play against your own incompetence, under the stern gaze of that fierce Scottish God. You may have tricks to put your opponent off, like being sick on the ball during his backswing (I'm glad I just thought of that), but it's not going to make your own drive an inch longer.

I think it was Nicklaus who complained, when the bigger American ball was introduced, that playing over Carnoustie it tended to be in the rough on both sides of the fairway.

I shall skip the noble game of shinty because, while golf drives men to a despairing death – some of them – shinty merely guarantees for all a lifetime of plaster casts, and I'm talking about the spectators.

We return to fitba', which I simply do not understand. I support Partick Thistle. And *there's* stoic pessimism for you.

The Jags fan has raised to a degree unique in the world the talent for facing disaster square on, and when the team wins (it sometimes does, honestly), he responds like the Scottish farmer gazing out at gran' growing weather and muttering, "Aye, we'll pey for this . . .".

Supporters of other teams, it has to be faced, are capable of more dedicated partisanship, though Scotland has been left far behind in the form of looniness by other lands it would be a pity to name. One can, however, readily accept the experience of a priest who came upon a small crowd staring at a desperate character preparing to leap off a bridge parapet to his death. The cleric approached him cautiously to dissuade him. After some fruitless toing-and-froing he had an inspiration and exhorted him to stay alive for the sake of Celtic. He didn't support Celtic. For Rangers, then. (The priest was no bigot.) He didn't support Rangers.

"In that case jump, you useless atheist."

The basic truth is, of course, that our great institution of football isn't really about players. It's about fans and their fine madness, and the game itself is just a pretext for that madness.

"Yella card between eleven an' midnight, red card efter."

"Ye've been playin' that flamin' golf fur years an' years an'
never wance huv ye brung hame seventy thoosan' flamin'
quid!"

"He could be a champion once he learned to be bad tempered, ill mannered and rude."

"If there's wan thing ah'm dreadin' it's the second round."

"Me an' him's startin' a John McEnroe Supporters Club, are ye jinin?'

"Come an' change channels fur me, hen, in case a pu' a hamstring."

"When does the Open shut?"

"Ah think it's ridic'lous you gettin' a new hat every year."

"The name's Ballesteros. Andra Ballesteros."

"Funny ye never hear aboot a sheep wi' a horseskin noseband."

"Ye never hear Jack Nicklaus moanin' aboot havin' tae use an iron."

"He's a great Ian Botham fan."

"Can they no' get a new course tae play oan?"

"If ye've tae keep yer head doon when ye're playin' golf how dae ye see where ye're goin'?"

"An' always remember tae reserve enough energy tae jump up an' doon punchin' the air should ye happen tae win."

"The only time ah've saw you runnin' as hard as that wa the day yon man offered ye a joab!"

"An' remember, don't start sprintin' until the last five miles."

"Jist when ah wis thinkin' aboot goin' in fur it tae."

"Awfu' worried, doctor. He wants tae play fitba' instead of just throwin' beer cans like normal boys!"

"She's the number one seed because she won the jackpot last week."

"Awfu' pleased wi hersel' ... done her personal best the night."

"Ah suppose if the Australians beat us they'll be under the moon."

"If it wisnae fur the bingo an' the bettin' shop this place wid be a cultural desert."

"If ye won half a million on the pools wid ye still want tae see a more equal distribution o' wealth?"

"Ye'd better lay aff the Valium in case they huv a dope test at the bingo."

"That yin's caused enough bother in cricket withoot bringin' him intae the fitba'."

"There's nothing wrong with your husband that a couple of wins for Rangers wouldn't put right."

"Ah wonder whit they're testin' him fur."

"Nice to see Mildred showing her athleticism."

"See if Maradona had been born in Springburn."

"They might huv gave us some snooker."

"See ma man? He wid be anither Georgie Best if he could play fitba."

"Ah asked his advice an' he said somethin' aboot keepin' control in the middle o' the park, tightenin' up ma defence an' tryin' tae score on the break."

"You are going to have the honour, my son, of being the world's first twenty-five bob player."

"O.K. Don't tell me! Instead o' comin' back through the iron curtain ye tried tae celebrate by jumpin' o'er it!"

"Aw well. Least said Souness mended."

"Couldnae get a ticket, so ah went tae the Chelsea Flooer Show an' got flung oot fur shoutin' at the Judges an' singin' 'The Flower o' Scotland'."

"Ah don't like the look o' this, Jimmy, the ref's sponsored by a firm o' spectacle manufacturers."

"Listen! Teeh total or no' teeh total ye'll wear the beer advert like the rest o' them."

"At least growin' oranges'll make a change fae curin' haddies."

"We're still lookin' for a sponsor."

"He's goin' early tae get acclimatised tae bawlin' an' shoutin' at high altitudes."

"Ah think it must be disc jockeys that's ridin' thae horses ah back."

"Ah've always said it should be included in the Olympic Gemmes."

"Ye know spring's jist roon the corner when that Budd appears."

"And for viewers with black and white sets the next ball I am going to pot is a sort of pale shade of sweetie pink."

"Ah jist want a shampoo an' set."

"Here, ah like yer trainers, Agnes, whit are ye trainin' fur?"

"Looks as if old Gatting's been caught in the slips bowling a maiden over."

"Surely there must be an easier way tae get Wembley tickets than supportin' Tranmere Rovers."

"Whit d'ye mean he's no' a patch oan Lester Piggott!"

"Makes ye wish ye had taken up golf, Albert."

"Nae wonder he comes hame ravin' aboot seein' bogeys, birdies an' eagles an' that."

"He's jist heard aboot gallopin' inflation an' he's checkin' up tae see whit race it's in."

HOLIDAYS

Oh, the joy of getting away from it all. I once knew a young fellow, and this is a true story, who realised that the end of the rainbow was somewhere else – Paris, in his case. He was sick and tired of the sheer awful provincialism of Scotland, he was bored to death and he spent quite a lot of time boring us to death about it too. Everything would be different in Paris, city of light, where poets and artists wolfed *vin blanc* at pavement cafés, sorted out the universe and then retired to garrets to produce masterpieces with the encouragement of a ravishing French doll or two.

Now the only snag about this man's dream is that when you flit to Paris, you can leave behind the grimy Gorbals and the nagging neighbours and the cloying Kelvinside conventionality. What you can't leave behind is yourself, and this guy was going to be exactly the same boring poultice in Montmartre as he was in Maryhill.

Depressing, isn't it? Well, life is real and life is earnest, and the gravy is our goal, it says somewhere, I think, so let's put a brave face on it and be as miserable as hell. That's probably good for the soul.

On the other hand, it can be a dilly. If we don't happen to be as dreary as my friend, we still have to export our crazy, mixed-up personalities as essential baggage when we wave ta-ta to the Broomielaw or Abbotsinch, and that essential baggage is the fun of it all. When I refer to essential baggage I am not thinking of the wife, but on second thoughts I am thinking of her as well.

So there's some corner of a foreign field that is forever Glesca. Being essentially open-minded and open-hearted people, we do absorb and welcome the quaint cultural variations of our holiday destinations. (Open-handed is right, incidentally. In former days, if a Glaswegian got back to Central Station from the Fair Fortnight on the Isle of Man and discovered that he still had enough loose change for the bus fare home, he felt he must

have cheated somebody.)

We are deeply impressed that some kids can speak good Spanish at the age of four, suspecting as we do that the Spanish speak that strange lingo only in our presence – to impress us – and lapse into ordinary talk when they're alone.

We take to strange dishes as if we ate them to a band playing back home, because of course we do. Did you ever hear of a Scots restaurant in Glasgow among the trattorias and Greek joints and Chinky cairry-oots? So we are the playboys and playgirls of the western world, getting tore in with the chopsticks and gobbling Continental breakfasts when we know that mankind was designed to start the day on ham and eggs or a brisk cuppa and a daud of dry toast.

Holidays are therefore a very wild experience for the Glaswegian, and his essential baggage, since she is sometimes more inclined to broaden her wee toty mind with overseas cultures than is her Jimmy. That may be why Majorca is absolutely infested with Glesca-style pubs and wee places that go in for fish suppers with a lot of vinegar.

The Hanleys have made their own contribution to this wild invasion. We once drove through France to Northern Spain, and daughter Jo, who was about 12, had this dedicated urge to find the best chips in Continental Europe. She lived on chips, and did quite well.

The French illiterates do not put vinegar on chips, would you believe? In one wee French town we went into a restaurant, or restarong, where the chips came high on her list, but she asked for vinegar, and the only thing they had was wine vinegar. Okay, okay.

So we had the north of Spain, and on the way back we went into the same restaurant. Suddenly! Everybody in that wee town was ordering huge plates of chips and smothering them with wine vinegar. Glasgow had made one of its great cultural exports. Chips with vinegar.

That wine vinegar costs a bomb but it is very superior stuff. In my young days we would go to the chemist's shop and buy a wee bottle of acetic acid, a substance that would dissolve your tongue in a wanny, but when grossly diluted became vinegar. Never mind malt, never mind wine, glacial acetic acid slipped into a pint of water brought chips to life and made your hair grow, in several directions.

So we take our own weird culture to those faraway places with strange-sounding names. We take ourselves. Apart from the waiters and these weans who can speak foreign gibberish, we never meet anybody except other tourists whose patter takes us back to Partick or Paisley, since these are the places where all the real people live.

Chip shops proliferate, and try saying that after a couple of bottles of plonk. Go on. We go abroad, and some desperate young blokes go a broad, which nowadays one cannot recommend. We go abroad, we mix, we settle into European culture, and we remain ourselves, we can't throw off our essential baggage. I was going to say we add to the gaiety of nations, except that gaiety has a bad name nowadays. I used to be gay, now I am merely merry, and I hope nobody spoils that word either.

We often get it wrong. What a good idea. Getting it wrong is a lot of the fun, as you will find in succeeding pages. The Glaswegian abroad tends to be, and I grope for the definition . . . rawther Glaswegian. See me? See ma man? See Spain? See hoalidays? Eh, Hablo Espagnol, Jaime? Chips wi'vinegar, por favor.

"Just imagine the hold-up, sir, if everyone returning from Benidorm were to kiss the tarmac."

"Whit d'ye expect on a cheap, economy flight, a ravin' beauty?"

"Hijack or no hijack, ah object tae bein' body searched on the Largs/Millport ferry."

"Me an' Wullie's reciprocatin' by visitin' Benidorm at the Ferr."

"That young lassie wis me before ah joined the back o' yer flamin' queue."

"We always come tae Blackpool — Majorca's too commercialised!"

"Jist imagine how bad it wid be if this wisnae mid-summer!"

"Have you any cheap package holidays which are not described as cheap package holidays?"

"Marvellous, i'ntit ... no' near as heavy as last summer."

"The row's no' about the delays it's about the programmes they want tae watch."

"We've discovered a wee Chinese restaurant that sells smashin' fish suppers!"

"Diz ony o' youse yins talk English?"

"Typical, i'ntit! We've jist won a fortnight's holiday fur two in the Falklands."

"We'r fur Saltcoats again, Alec, whit aboot yersel'?"

"Ye canny whack the wide open spaces, sure ye canny?"

"That's their bad luck, we don't go hame till a week come Saturday!"

"He disnae fancy a Caribbean cruise an' ah don't fancy a week self-caterin' in Girvan so whit huv ye got in between?"

"We're no' daft, Wullie ... back tae work jist in time tae get wan fur wur ain holidays."

"Come oan, hurry up! Yer ice cream's getting' cauld!"

"That's wan thing aboot comin' tae Coatbrig' fur wur Easter holidays, we've nae trouble wi' ile slicks an' that!"

"Actually, we feel quite at home here, having venetian blinds in our bungalow at Giffnock."

"Ah've been tae Benidorm thousan's o' times an' the only thug ah've ever seen wis this wan ah took wi' me."

"He says he canny hear his transistor fur the ither transistors!"

"Ah think wimmen look ridiculous in thae hot pants!"

"Me an' him's huvin' a rerr terr learnin' wur waiter how fur tae talk English an' that."

"Haw, Jessie, ah didnae know this is whit they meant by room with bath, balcony an' sea view."

"Cancel wur holidays tae the Costa Brava. If the Rangers disnae go intae Europe neither dae we!"

"Ah'll be glad when this summer's past an' ah can see daylight again."

"Ye've got tae compete, so ah gie them paella fur their breakfast, spaghetti bolognese fur their dinner an' moussaka fur their tea."

"And to think we went and came to Largs because you said Majorca was too common."

"Magic holiday ... ma nose is skint, ma back's skint an' he's skint!"

"Ah think you'd better see it this time, Angus, ah saw it last time."

"Their holiday video's even more borin' than their holiday snapshops used tae be."

"Of *course* it's rotten! Whit dae ye expect when we've had nae practice since last September?"

"Aye, we've went an' cancelled wur holidays in Spain an' we're goin' tae the Costa Brava instead."

"Typical, i'ntit, prepare fur a long wait an' ye take aff on time."

"Ah don't care if the Russians ARE pullin' out ah'm no' goin' tae Afghanistan fur ma holidays."

"Ah wis jist goin' doon tae Largs fur the day but a bargain's a bargain, i'ntit?"

"Ah suppose if God had meant us tae fly he wid huv invented air traffic controllers that didnae go on strike."

"Congratulations, sir! You are our ten thousandth passenger to be held up for more than six hours and have won our free bottle of tranquillisers."

"Tricky wan here, Brian. Have we got anything without sun drenched beaches, azure blue seas an' romantic midnight barbecues?"

"Excuse me, but are we allowed tae sit doon when we're oan stand-by?"

"Ah've heard aboot the Highland Board but ah never thought ah'd huv tae sleep on it!"

"Gets terrible bored daein' nuthin' efter a few days, misses bein' oan strike at hame."

"Hide the aspirins, Andra, ah think it's the Drug Squad."

"How dae ye expect me tae relax when ah've went an' forgot the Spanish fur Valium?"

"Take thae sun-glasses aff till ah see where ye're lookin'!"

"You might ca' it men's lib — ah ca' it disgustin'!"

"Is that you, Wullie, or is it somebody else?"

"She says something aboot passengers fur somewhere on flight number something report tae gate number something else immediately."

"It's a'right fur you, you're jist goin' tae Mosspark — ah'm goin' tae Yugo-Slavia."

"With each Spanish holiday we reserve floor space on the airport lounge complete with sleeping bag and calendar."

"Could ye make it a double-decker, hen, this yin likes his smoke?"

"Right! Altogether now. 'The train to Spain is quicker than the plane'."

"Terrible cauld ootside, can ah staun' beside yer bills fur a wee while?"

"Are ye sure Munich has fabulous beaches, blue Mediterranean seas an' Flamenco dancers?"

'Ectually we've trevelled so widely that we find it easier to convert from Pounds to Dollars, to Lira, to Yen and THEN to Pesetas."

"How is it ye spend a' year as a flyin' picket an' then ye're feart tae go yer holidays in an airyplane?"

"Rothesay, an' ah don't want wan o' thae hotels that's no'
built yet!"

"As a shareholder, ah demand a shot at drivin' ma airyplane."

"A fine time tae run oot o'petrol."

"Ah didnae know it wis fur men only."

POSH

The Almighty must love scruff, because He made so many of them. He did, did He not? And you can name a dozen of them without even looking up your notebook. This place is packed with them.

There is a curious myth that there is no such thing as snobbery in the Glasgow area, and I have actually contributed to it, because I sometimes get blind, like other people I meet in the gutter. Ach, snobbery is the game, and it's a great game.

Favourite true story I got from the late Eric de Banzie. A West End Glasgow lady was travelling to the toon by bus, and was aware that a female person, presumably a char, was sitting behind her with a grandwean on her knee. One has to put up with such creatures if one wants one's kitchen floor scrubbed. The wean was chowing an orange, and as the bus trundled down Highburgh Road, the lady became conscious of an acid odour, and realised that the brat was rubbing the orange experimentally on her fur coat collar. Before she could deliver a crushing remark, the scruffy person chid the child: "Stoap that, you'll get your orange aw herry."

Let us move the scene to Edinburgh, which does cheerfully admit to a certain separation of the proles from the People. A Corstorphine lady was window-shopping at Jenner's (why do Edinburgh ladies keep buying windows?) when she became aware of a low-class wummin-type person staring at her. She ignored the creature, of course, but she couldn't abolish her, and the wummin finally solved a mystery, leapt forward and cried, "You're Mrs McCaggerty from Wester Hailes!"

The reply was totally crushing. "Quite the contrary."

Move back to Glasgow, and we luxuriate in the magic of snobbery. I spent my infancy in the Gallowgate, but went to school in Dennistoun, which involved walking along an enormous pedestrian bridge over the railway. The Gallowgate was definitely downmarket, as my brutal teacher Miss Coutts was eager to tell me while she bashed me with the pointer to

prove her social superiority over tiny scruff weans.

Even in the Gallowgate, it was okay to live in Cubie Street, but one block eastward, Soho Street was definitely right down the social scale. Cubie Street wasn't exactly posh, but see, compared with Soho Street? Aristocratic, Jimmy.

So we moved to Sandyhills, a wee Corporation housing scheme farther east, built between the old villages of Tollcross and Shettleston. Ah, magic. Baths. Hot water. Gardens. Snobbery. I didn't fancy the bath bit, but okay, we were superior.

Then some schoolmates found the scheme was divided by the Tollcross Burn, running east to west, and insisted that only their families, to the south, lived in Sandyhills. Us scruff to the north of the burn lived in Shettleston. See, one arrangement of letters is higher-class than another.

The unfortunate schoolmates who actually lived in Shettleston, up tenement closes with no running H and C, told us that hot baths softened the spine. The great thing about snobbery is that you can turn it upside down and it still makes what sense it wants to.

Snobbery in Greenock? Greenock, for heaven's sake? Oh, take my word for it. When actor Roy Hanlon graduated to Greenock High School, he let it be known that they lived in the West End of the town. Some boring rat-finks trailed him home and accused him of living in the East End. Always quick on the draw, he pointed out that his tenement close was actually in Central Greenock. (You get the subtleties here, I'm sure. Having no acquaintance with Greenock except as a main street on the way to Gourock, I am baffled.)

The same man used to be taken on visits to an aunt on the East Coast, of whom he stood in great awe when he found that she was the acknowledged leader of the social set in Kirkcaldy. See the New York 700? See debutantes? No, don't. See Kirkcaldy.

Ah, the Scots are the great egalitarians, it says in a book I read somewhere. Some are more equal than others. Some are just plain scruff. Some of us, on the other hand, are fairly high-class. We eat lemming sole and chips. And we never sook the paper after a fish supper. One has certain social obligations, does one no? I meant nut. I mean no. Hivvings, I nearly gave away my humble origins there. But I have rose abune them, and don't any of youse dare mention my Auntie Sarah or I shall have my hubby ram this cakestand up your scruffy nose.

"Thinks she's a flamin' superstar because they put the
damp walls in her Cooncil hoose on the telly."

"This Stenley Bexter seems to be quate clever but I don't understend his Glesgow petter. Efter all quate a lot of us Glesgow people talks proper!"

"Haw, Agnes, wumman lookin' fur some place ca'd The Berrows where they sell china dogs an' haun' knitted fryin' pans..."

"If ah had a Rolls Royce ah doobt ah'd be changin' it fur somethin' wee'er, wid you no', Agnes?"

"Of course, ah wid never huv went an' mairrit Prince Charles in the first place, wid you, Alice?"

"V.A.T. on books widnae worry me, ah've already got a book."

"One doesn't mind crude oil as long as it's not pornographic."

"It jist seems like yesterday that our biggest worry wis whether or no' tae vote for Roy Jenkins."

"How d'you fency stuffing your money down a hole in the grun', Morag?"

"Our choice this year was between the Seychelles and Tighnabruaich and, as we're both passionately fond of midges, we've plumped for Tighnabruaich."

"And remember, Norman, we're not to be seen looking at cars under the £20,000 price range."

"I wish a cold one to heat in my micro-wave oven."

"Obviously, my dear, if one joins a Common Market one expects to encounter common people."

"Ah like yer new rig-oot, Elsie. Whit boutique did ye get it oot o'?"

"Unfortunately, Norman has had to stop buying me red roses in case people think we're socialists."

"If ah jined the Sloane Rangers wid ma man huv tae gie up his season ticket at Parkhead?"

"Course, we have our Venetian blinds direct from Venice."

TELLY

I once wrote a snippet for a television series in which a wife was glued to the telly while her husband read the racing pages, and she said with great excitement, "A terrific programme, Willie – it's a wifie watching a married couple on TV, and she's telling her man it's a terrific programme . . .".

In the early days of the medium, another writer predicted that the Americans would willingly elect a Scotch terrier to the Presidency if it kept appearing on the box. See power?

My late mother, when she was living on her own, was picture-daft. She would go to the State or the Odeon three or four times a week in any weather, and when I gave her a present of a wee 13-inch Murphy she said she wouldn't have the thing in the house. After two days she abandoned the State and the Odeon and moved her easy chair to get a square-on view.

There used to be a wee interval feature showing two windows endlessly turning through each other. It hypnotised her. Everything hypnotised her. And she saved a lot of admission money, of course, while going into a permanent cheerful daze.

Ah, where would we be without it? Out robbing banks like normal people, maybe. And it's probably true about that Scotch terrier. I once did another programme where I just sat staring straight into the camera and blethered about anything that came up my humph. It went out late on a Friday, and hot-blooded men would stop me on the street and complain that they couldn't get their wives to bed till the flaming Hanley programme was finished. Oh, power indeed.

The point is that if I had gone into a pub and started to blether solo for 15 minutes, the customers would have fled, including the women – some of them might have let me have one with the handbag first. I mean, is Derek Jameson real? The viewers will swallow anything as long as it's *there*.

Parties to a divorce don't squabble much about the custody of weans; just about who gets the box. It's the end of civilisation as we know it, of course. It was clear from the start to expert sociologists that it would kill the art of conversation. Well, listen, Jimmy, while I talk to you solo for a minute. I was in a lot of houses before anybody dreamed up John Logie Baird, and in some of them an evening's glittering conversation consisted of four or five harrumphs and a "Whit?".

When the great new medium arrived, it actually brought conversation with it. Like:

"Will you look at that lassie's blouse? It's disgustin'."

"I never noticed, I'm tryin' tae make oot whit she's sayin."

"See men!"

Not sparkling, maybe. But better than five harrumphs and a whit.

Actually, there used to be regular letters to the papers complaining about half-naked lassies and steamy sex scenes that hid nothing. I'm telling you, I went through the channels like a ferret, but I must have had the wrong make of set. Or maybe they only got that stuff in Wales.

Obviously, it puts illicit desires in viewers' minds, as Mrs Whitehouse has assured us, though it doesn't put any in *her* mind. And censors are immune to temptation, of course, which is why they love their job so much. It's a known historical fact that nobody ever even thought of extra-marital nooky till the BBC brainwashed them.

And there's a well-attested case of a man who watched *Bill and Ben* incessantly, and went out and committed a parking offence.

So just watch it. Whit? Oh, you're already watching it. Anything dirty, I hope?

"When ah wis your age we had tae make wur ain boredom!"

"Dampt disgrace payin' yer licence money an' havin' tae
wait till efter nine fur the sex an' violence."

"Thae home computers are spoilin' family life. He should be watchin' this late night horror movie."

"Can ah get walkin' past the television at half-time?"

"Ah'm glad ah didnae bother tae take doon thur black-out curtains in 1945."

"How much longer have ah tae suffer the humiliation o' goin' oot intae the world an' admittin' tae all an' sundry that we huvnae got a video?"

"An' don't come runnin' back tae me if yer mother's telly breaks doon."

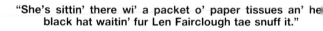

"She's sittin' there wi' a packet o' paper tissues an' he black hat waitin' fur Len Fairclough tae snuff it."

"Now, there's whit ah call a cultural breakthrough."

"Like ma Krystal Carrington peenie, Isa?"

"He got fed up wi' a' the violence so he smashed it up."

"The cauld weather has ended an' Dallas has started, is life no' wonderful!"

"A special Breakfast Television model, Madame, incorporating marmalade jar holder, toast-rack and cornflake container."

"Ah keep tryin' tae remember whit excuse ye had fur no' talkin' tae me before we had the telly."

"Hey, mastermind! There's a couple o' men fae the B.B.C. askin' if ye can remember when ye last bought a T.V. licence."

"An' ye can cut oot the 'Here we go, here we go, here we go', it's only a flamin' cricket match."

"Culturewise he's a lot better ... watches the snooker instead o' the darts."

"She likes that J.R. Carrington in 'Take The High Road', sure ye do, Effie?"

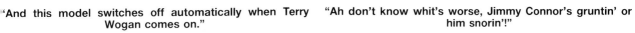

"And this model switches off automatically when Terry Wogan comes on."

"Ah don't know whit's worse, Jimmy Connor's gruntin' or him snorin'!"

"Brian blames the media fur everything, sure ye dae, Brian?"

"Of course ah'll marry ye, Brian, any day except 29th July when ah'll be watchin' the telly."

"Terrible yer man losin' his joab, Mrs Wilson ... we've had even worse luck, wur video's went on the blink."

"Ah don't want a video recorder tae record programmes .. ah want a video recorder before her next door gets wan."

"Ah fail tae see whit pleasure ye'll get lookin' at Selina Scott first thing in the mornin'."

"Never mind the sound as long as it's got more layers than their's next door."

"Whit's this we're watchin', Dallas or Dynasty?"

"Love-Fifteen, yer tea's no' ready, Love-Thirty — !"

'Of course ah blame the television for crime an' budgets."

"It used tae be jist square eyes, noo it's square eyes wi' coloured dots."

"There's somethin' wrang wi' wur telly ... ah switched oan an' Terry Wogan wisnae there."

"An' whit's even worse, they say Stan Ogden's havin' it off wi' Elsie Tanner."

"And if you think the news was bad wait till you hear the weather forecast."

"Ah reckon that's wimmen's biggest deal since the Suffragettes."

GRAPE

The grape, that can with logic absolute
The two-and-seventy jarring sects confute
The subtle alchemist that in a trice
Life's leaden metal into gold transmute

It's bad for us, of course. Contrary to popular illusion, alcohol is not a stimulant, but a depressant. It lowers the activity of the forward sections of the brain, the bits that contain the self-critical faculty, and on practically any Friday evening we can hear a pint-sized Glaswegian explaining that very scientific fact to his mates in the corner.

They don't listen a lot, of course, and the vowels sometimes tend to be slurred because of the turbulence of the pub floor caused by the passing subway train several miles away. It tends to vibrate the lower jaw and puts a lot of undulating teeth in the way of the tongue.

In any case, one of the mates is simultaneously explaining that cigarettes are not a relaxant, as popular myth would have it, but a stimulant, virtually jagging needles into the adrenal glands and producing enough sheer exuberance to cut the four-minute mile to 40 seconds.

The two other mates are not paying a lot of attention to this vital information either, though one of them is thinking, in a confused manner, that if all this is true, a drinking man should keep up with the fags, because booze and nicotine cancel each other out. Balance, balance, that is the game.

Do you drink a lot? No, I spill most of it. I am too drunk to face the wife. I am also too sober to face the wife. I shall go over the top and have a pony of alcohol-free lager. Inspiring, bold John Barleycorn! What dangers thou canst make us scorn! Wi' tippenny, we fear nae evil; wi' usquebae, we'll face the devil! And so on and so on, of course.

The Glaswegian has a particular attitude to the booze. He is particular about whose round it is, for instance, and it's usually his, again. He is very pernickety about his favourite brand of whisky, though after five halfs he couldn't tell Teacher's from turpentine. It is all a part of the great ritual, a device to release the inhibited Einsteinian IQ from its wee prison somewhere near the back of the neck .

There has been a social revolution, of course. In respectable times, Glasgow pubs would have a sort of secluded shrine labelled the Ladies' Room, where female persons, sometimes accompanied by their male persons, would get quietly smashed without being observed by the scruffy regulars. Today, women will actually stand at a bar as if they were full human beings. Some will even utter reckless words like tut-tut and bring a blush to the innocent cheek of the blotto keelie beside them. The Calvinistic world of Glasgow is going to rack and ruin.

Some years go, my bank manager invited me to lunch, because he was getting so much fun out of my overdraft, and since I had a joint account, he included my wife, and brought his too. Invited to have a pre-prandial tipple, his wife fancied a wee whisky. My wife asked for a hauf and a hauf, and Johnny's wife fair lit up as she begged for the same. She had been trying to look perjink till she realised she was among genuine scruff who would not sneer. It was a good lunch, though I don't remember the food much.

The important thing is that in the boozer, we can put up with people who would be intolerable if we were sober. And maybe more important, they can put up with us. It is not without significance that Noah (yes, the one with the boat) kept himself fairly well guttered during those 40 days. It helped him to tolerate all those dinosaurs and boll weevils as well as the wife and weans, and one can only hope there were licensed premises on Mount Ararat when they arrived there. If not, he probably built a family department from the timbers of the ark, and re-established civilisation as we know it.

It is bad for you. But in Glasgow, when it brings out the worst in us, that can look and sound a lot more tolerable than the best in us. When we're good, we can be awfy tedious. When we're bad, we nearly resemble human beings.

Well, that's my story. What's yours? And if you answer "a double brandy" you will kindly leave the pub.

"Norman's going in for wine making in a big way."

"Funny, i'ntit, when ye're wee ye want a bucket an' spade an' when ye're big a' ye want's a bucket!"

"That's right, sir, we're a wine bar.... sell everything bar wine."

"Huv you been re-shufflin' this cabinet again?"

"O.K., ah can go hame noo, ah'm unwound."

"— But whit's the matter wi' Strathclyde 'cause it's goin' round an' round?"

"Nice tae get a breath o' sea air fur the last wee holiday o' the year, i'ntit?"

"Jist because ye arrived two days late there's nae need tae try an' catch up."

"If the watter workers come oot we'll gie them wur moral support by takin' it neat, whit d'ye say, Hughie?"

"Right! That wis a bottle o' whisky, a bottle o' gin an' a bottle o' vodka for strictly medicinal purposes. Next please!"

"Well, if they'll no' keep the pubs open later, we'll jist huv tae learn tae drink quicker."

"Huv yiz ony liminade an' crisps, hen?"

"D'ye ever wonder how they get that upside doon whisky intae the bottle, Wullie?"

"Aye, drooth's a terrible thing — ma man's suffered fae it fur years!"

"We don't fancy the hoose but yer champagne's lovely."

"Walter's a great believer in makin' his ain."

"Typical! When they should be buildin' mare public houses!"

"I think it wis mixin' a' that whisky wi' non-alcoholic lager."

"See thae two Labour guys Haddock an' Kinersley....?"

"There's wan thing, naebody can lay the blame at your door."

"Oor Kevin goes tae practice twice a week at the tap o' Ben Nevis."

"Coal cellars in Maryhill wis never a patch oan beer cellars in Munich, Wullie!"

"We're fund raising to buy more cheese and wine for the next fund raising."

"Ah jist want it tae shake up an' doon an' skoosh in the event of ma winnin' something."

"Brilliant! Fried whisky fur wur breakfast, whisky casserole fur wur dinner an' grilled whisky fur wur tea."

FESTIVITIES

One year, around 2 January, a barmaid complained to me aboout customers coming in moaning about their hellish hangovers. "See Hogmanay?" she said. "It's strictly for amateurs."

But the Scot takes his festive seasons seriously, even glumly, though as the barmaid was aware the ancient traditions keep changing. Time was when Hogmanay was a day of strict abstinence. The man of the hoose might have a dram with his mates on the way home, but once there he had to be a good boy and enter the New Year sober, clean and virtuous. The bottle stood on the dresser along with the shortbread and black bun, and his eyes would stray to it speculatively, but it belonged to a year that hadn't come yet, and it was sacred.

The house was polished and cleaned to death. There used to be queues on Hogmanay at Cooncil offices and other places, of good citizens waiting to pay any due bills and slough off debt to face Ne'erday clear. And of course at five minutes to the witching hour the ashes would be cleaned out of the coal fire and taken down to the midding – toffee-nosed husbands would take them in a briefcase, of course.

The minutes took years to pass till the bells struck the first note and the boats down at the Clyde went mad with their hooters. Dad went mad with a large hoot, and mum burst out greeting. Always. It was suddenly a time to remember things past, and friends lost or far away. Maybe it was a catharsis, whatever that is.

Maybe the old man sat and waited for the first foot. Maybe he leapt out to first-foot somebody himself. The night, where I lived, was full of citizens both bottle in hand, greeting other citizens and sharing a toast, and turning up at the wrong house. It didn't matter. On New Year's Morning, if there was a lighted room, anybody was welcome . Everyone forgave their enemies, buried old feuds, or had a decent stab at it. Some people vanished for days. The world was renewed, prime and flawless, and it would even feel like it for a few days.

Maybe it had something to do with the Balder legend of brief rebirth and renewal after the cold miserable northern winters. Who cares? It's for fun, even if we can't actually drain the central heating system and flood the midgie-can nowadays.

Kids even used to get their presents on Neerday. Christmas was a newfangled and suspicious notion. The whole thing's ruined now, of course. The brats get their big Christmas hoolie and then have the cheek to stay up for the New Year bells forbye. The world's in a state of chassis.

Well, all right. We can either have a week of sobriety between the two festivals or just have enough drams in between to create a merger of celebrations.

Birthdays can get a bit boring when they've been happening for long enough, but the shock can be minimised by a hefty swig of the cratur.

The other big one is Burns' birthday, of course, and it can be worth jouking this because the planet is infested with a lot of people dragging up weary old jokes worn to death by the centuries. It can have its moments, as when an orator at the Bridgeton Burns Club had a completely new twist and went through a litany of the *other* great Scots who should also be celebrated — the inventors, the philosophers, the medicos, the lot. "Now," he declaimed, "do any of you go out and deliberately get drunk on the birthday of John Loudon Macadam?"

As he paused for dramatic effect, a wee guy at the end of the table squinted round at him and garbled, "Aye, probably!"

This response could catch on among ingenious Scots. Just think of the length of the list. The very brain recoils, as it does so often in this great country, with a bit of help from a tumbler.

"Whit office party? Ye don't work in an office!"

"Jist whit ah needed, an executive bleedin' briefcase!"

"Ma man kisses me under the mistletoe at Christmas an'
under protest fur the rest o' the year."

"Remember the smashin' parties we used tae have when
the office wis staffed by people?"

"An' don't give me that stuff aboot inflation, V.A.T., the Gross National Product etc.!"

"Dae we want tae watch ten minutes o' carols on video, 50p?"

"A bottle o' dry sherry an' two bottles o' wet sherry!"

"He's reliable, ma man! Cairrit hame at half past twelve every year, regular's the clock!"

"Merry Christmas, hen, an' ah hope Santa brings the B.M.W. in the colour ye asked fur."

"Funny, i'ntit ... ye spend twenty quid on fast food an' it takes ye half-an-hour tae get through the check-out."

"Nice tae get back tae normal efter a' the festivities, i'ntit, Jimmy."

"Isn't liminade a terrible price this year, Agnes?"

"Tae tell ye the truth, Isa, ah'll be glad when ah've stoaped enjoyin' masel'."

"No' bein' included in the New Year Honours List disnae seem tae worry him."

"We're huvin' mince wi' bread sauce, cranberry sauce an' stuffin'."

"Ye didnae bring me what ah wanted last year — as a matter o' fact ah'm still single!"

"As it's the thought that counts, whit's yer cheapest?"

"We're gathered here fur tae honour the man that wrote poetry wance a year on 25th January."

"Did ye ever get the feelin' that ye had an economic crisis comin' oan!"

"Say when!"

"Dae ah look like somebody that could crash a gate?"

"I expect we'll have our usual quota of once-a-year people who think Coward was the first Noel."

"Ah want a go-slow train set."

"Hey, Jessie, are ye sure ye gave the dustmen their Christmas tip?"

"Am ah puttin' you doon fur a Porsche 924 or a perr o' socks?"

"Now that my mum's got loads o' credit cards she reckons you're redundant."

"An' ask him tae leave his sledge an' reindeers when he's finished wi' them!"

"We're huvin' a real plastic tree this year, no' an auld green wan that grows in a field!"

"Right! Oot wi' the cheque book, ah know ye're in there somewhere."

"Typical! 'Wishing you a Happy Valentine's Day and a Merry Christmas when it comes'."

"Ye're away tae propose the Immortal Memory but tomorrow mornin' ye'll no' even can remember where ye've been."

"We don't often sing 'Good King Wenceslas' at Easter."

"Instead o' Christmas cards this year we're sendin' beggin' letters!"

"Ma man's no' buyin' me a fur coat this year. Whit's your man no' buyin' ye?"

EATING OUT

The observer of mature years naturally has a twinge of nostalgia for a simpler age, when eating out was a proley affair, alternating between the occasional Macallum at the Tally's and the fish supper at the place next door. And even more essential to the true historic spirit of Scotland, having the same fish supper and eating out right on the street, using fingers, which have a longer nobler history than knives and forks, and ritually sooking the paper at the end to get the last dregs of the sauce and vinegar.

The observer of mature years or, if you prefer, the boring old poultice, may be forgiven since he has after all lived through a revolution nearly as shattering as that wee experience the Tsars had to suffer, and his old world has vanished like a puff of bubble gum.

It isn't only the package holidays, though they have had their insidious influence. The Scot has just got used to getting his feet below the table away from the but-and-ben, something that in his childhood he merely dreamed of when he saw it happening to William Powell and Myrna Loy. And in any case, of course, there is a completely new generation, the boring young poultices, who grew up taking it for granted that you took a bird out to an actual restaurant and jammed her with food and drink in the hope of lowering her resistance to your evil advances.

A far cry from Wendy's Tearoom and Miss Craig's, sighs the boring old poultice. Get tore in there, cries the boring young poultice.

But who would have believed it? The very first Chinese restaurant in Glasgow opened away back about 1950 and was regarded as fairly weird because it was in a Govan tenement, and without knocking Govan in any way, it was hardly regarded as being in the *avantgarde* of sophisticated advance. The management was not daft, though. It offered a choice between the exotic dishes of the Orient and more recognisable fare like totties and mince for the cautious proles of the area. Thus it

lured them in and launched them into the new era.

You may protest that the city already had exotic *haute cuisine* in places like the Rogano and the Royal and Ferrari's. Okay, but they were in the toney city centre catering for the hoi-polloi, a body which I just succeeded in joining by lying about my age.

I lied about other things too. Lunching with a Swiss acquaintance in Ferrari's (one of the noblest eateries in Europe), I plumped for steak tartare. My companion looked slightly askance and asked me if I knew what it was. Of course I knew what it was, I said. I didn't shilly-shally, I told a straightforward lie. Then it came, and I realised I would have to eat this frightening plate of raw mince to safeguard my reputation.

Well, I'm glad I decided to live dangerously and pave the way for coming generations to get tore in at raw mince and learn to knit jumpers from vermicelli and spatter goulash on the carpets and remove the roofs of their mouths with curry. Chopsticks were for ignorant peasants, of course. So we nearly went to night-school to get lessons in the primitive art. We probably made awful fools of ourselves.

And what a good idea. We can still make terrible fools of ourselves eating out, and wouldn't life be dull if we couldn't?

"Ah'll huv ma Continental Breakfast fae a continent where they get bacon, sausages, eggs, tamatas an' black puddin'."

"Whit's this then, Jimmy, meals on wheels or à la cart?"

"The soup's vegetable wi' hydrolised protein, monosodium glutamate, emulsifier, colouring, citric acid an' antioxidant."

"That was a lovely meal, please convey my compliments to the herbalist."

"I'm sorry, sir, we don't serve ploughmen."

"Whit wine dae ye recommend tae go wi' tough steak, hard peas an' cauld chips?"

"Y.O.P. jist sent me tae be a waitress, they didnae say nuthin' aboot smilin'."

"Ah never saw nuthin' on the telly aboot a waitress's go-slow, did you?"

"Ah don't mind the canned music, it's the canned soup ah object tae."

"A curried fish supper, Mac!"

Somebody's been tamperin' wi' this chicken, it tastes like chicken."

"These yins want wan chicken in the basket, wan scampi in the basket an' wan tamata soup in the basket."

Do you wish a dry wine or one that's just slightly damp?"

"We're oan grouse, egg an' chips the night, whit are youse huvin'?"

"Mince for both, medium rare."

"The soup o' the day wis finished yesterday."

"When he asked how ye liked yer steak, did ye huv tae say 'minced'?"

"Russian Tea's AFF!!"

"An' fur goodness sake ask fur a take-away no' a curry oot."

"Would you like white cheese and red wine, red cheese and white wine, white cheese and white wine or red cheese and red wine?"

'Thae Chinese restaurants is springin' up 'a ower the place!'

"Never mind the first class cuisine, whit's the grub like?"

"Grouse an' chips in the basket fur two, hen."

"Even the monosodium glutamate's no' as good as it used tae be."

"The topless waitress didnae turn up!"

"Ah don't take sugar but, seein' it's scarce, ah'd better huv two spoonfu'!"

MARRIED BLISS

The family is the original battlefield, somebody very wise once said. It might have been myself. It's in the family that we learn to love people or hate people or envy people or bore people to death, or all of these things at once. Some people think the family itself is death, of course. In the fairy tales the hero finally gets the heroine and they live happily every after. In other words, the story is over, the adventures are all vanished. We hear no more of them and we don't want to.

Well, there must be some kind of life after death, because there are people walking the streets who got married years ago. Probably some of them are walking the streets *because* they got married years ago and they're frightened to go home and face the wife. They're too drunk to face the wife. Or they're too sober to face the wife.

Maybe that's more exciting than being nice, and dutiful, and understanding each other by telepathy and never exchanging a harsh word. I knew a wife who despaired because the man came home mirauc'lous every night and she bawled him out every night but to no avail. A neighbour wifie suggested using the gentle approach and smothering him with sweetness, so for want of a better idea, she did.

That night his slippers were warming by the fire and she helped him off with his coat and asked if he would like coffee or if he would prefer a dram. She was done up to the nines and wearing a diaphanous nightdress. He just boggled, and let her help him up to bed and get him ready. Then she lay beside him.

"Now," she said, "isn't this better than staying in the pub all night?"

"It's great. But ah'll get hell when ah get hame."

Life doesn't really stop, because there's always something happening. See men? See women? See them together? It isn't the same as the youthful romance full of dreams, though it can be quite nice if they learn to grit their teeth now and then.

The snag is that women are different from men. That's quite a good arrangement, actually, but it can be a snag as well. You see, men are practical, down-to-earth people, whereas women are romantic dreamers. Or vice versa, of course — in marriage you have to cover all the bets.

Division of labour is a good idea in the home, even intellectual labour, and it was a wise and kindly husband who proposed the wife should concentrate on the trivial things and he would worry about the big things. The trivial things would be like keeping the house and making the money last and paying the rent and cooking and so on. The big things the husband would take over would be worrying about the national debt and the situation in Beirut and the threat to the ozone layer.

What could be fairer or more generous?

The great thing about marriage is that the courting couple sometimes imagine that it will be a complete marriage of minds, they will know each other totally as if their brains had been siamesed.

Ha blooming ha, as it were. *Vive la difference*, as the hot-blooded Frenchman remarked, in French. A pair can be closer than peas in a pod, but there are two brains churning away in two separate skulls, and none of us knows exactly what is going on in there — there are too many wee cells working simultaneously.

So marriage, like everything else in human life, is a nicely crazy, mixed-up affair, and the family is the hotbed of everything from wild excitement to running head-first into granite. And in between, marvellous misunderstandings.

In other words, it's the jinkies.

"Jist like Dynasty, i'ntit, wi' flooers on the breakfast table."

"Ah wonder whit happened tae the wife swappin' parties."

"Ah suppose this is all part o' life's rich tapestry."

"Dae you realise that if there wis a nuclear war it wid be the end o' civilisation as we know it?"

"— But ah've already got a wee fat man wi' a tartan bunnet, a fag an' galluses."

"Listen! If ah say ye're jinin' the Human Rights Movement ye're jinin' the Human Rights Movement."

"Lucky devils, only eight years!"

"What should I wear with this, darling, my mink or my sheepskin?"

"See the price o' fags! Ah've had tae stoap the wife eatin' sweeties!!!"

"We decided on a patio...."

"How can we reach an agreement if ye refuse tae nego-
tiate?"

"Listen! If them next door huv a phone in the car we're
huvin' a phone in the car."

"Of course, we don't talk about conciliation now, we talk
about détente!"

"We've went an' fell oot again — ah say the weather's been
Arctic an' she says it's been Antarctic."

"Like it? Got it second haun' aff a British Caledonian stewardess."

"Ah don't know whit fur people need a pent house, can the no' keep their pent an' turps under the bed like everybody else."

"Listen! If ah say you're the head o' the household you're the head o' the household!!"

"That's fine! Ah'll away hame an' strike the wife!"

"Haw, Wullie, ye've jist got yersel' intae a Doomsday scenario."

"See the marriage contract! Ah don't think ah could huv read the small print."

"Are we no' supposed tae get mairrit first or somethin'?"

"The big balloon ah mairrit only manages tae float alang tae the pub."

"Ah reckon ye could get them under the Trade Description Act, Sophie."

"Dead keen on Animal Rights... refuses steaks or chops, jist sticks tae mince."

"O.K. So ye've got a blazer! Whit ah'm ah supposed tae dae, send fur the fire brigade?"

"Jist serve me ma tea! Ah don't care whether ye serve it fae the Royal Box end or the ither end!"

"Ma mother's no' in."

"Brian wants tae make a will leavin' me all his credit cards."

"Tell ye whit, fair's fair! You stop buyin' fags an' drink an'
ah'll stop buyin' motor caurs an' fur coats!"

"If yer mother's no' in try the wumman next door!"

"He comes in handy when we want tae keep a low profile."

"Ah gie him food containin' nae additives in case he gets hyper-active."

"That rainy day we saved up for has turned oot tae be a hurricane."

"Get this straight! As soon as this programme's feenished ah'm leavin' ye fur keeps!"

"No' shavin' for a couple o' days works wonders for his macho image."

"Listen! Wid ye tell thae cowboys that's mendin' yer roof tae stop tyin' their horses tae ma fence."

"Listen! Ah'm the wan that wears the troosers in this hoose!"

"Any newspaper wid pay a fortune fur a picture o' you goin' tae bed."

"If they offered me a thoosan' quid ah know wan union ah wid pack in."

"At least you don't need tae worry.... they don't huv tapes long enough tae take doon your telephone conversations."

"Why can ye no' learn tae talk sense like Joey?"

"Ye've always been repugnant but tae be redundant as well is the last straw."

"Ah don't care if it's Pancake Tuesday or Sheffield Wednes-day ye're huvin' pie an' beans as usual."

"That's that yin's man... A case o' Bridescake Revisited."

"Whit dae ah need tae dae tae get a kiss nooadays, score a goal?"

"Is it true ye're goin' tae refuse yer Giro wance they privatise it, Hughie?"

"There's livin' proof that they don't need tae spend a' that money on leisure centres."

"It's an artist wantin' ye tae pose fur a still life."

"Be fair, Sharon, EVERYBODY canny get their picturs on plates an' mugs jist because they're gettin' mairrit."

"Apart fae leavin' yer man whit else wid ye dae if ye won a million poun', Mrs McCallum?"

"Right, ye can huv yer bags packed an' oot o' here by 1992."

"Whit kind o' after shave dae ye want this year, Damask Rose, Peach Blossom, or Honeysuckle?"

"Ye neednae bother comin' back tae me, hen, ah'm jist leavin' yer faither."

"Me an' yer mother huv came tae a threshold agreement — she's no' allowed tae cross it!"

"His ambition wis tae go fae rags tae riches an', a' credit tae him, he's managed the first bit."

"Haw, Andra, will ye come an' tell me ma weight."

"An' you huvnae even scraped the surface o' the gairden yet!"

"Even if it suits the Duchess of York it disnae necessarily suit you."

"Why must you insist on callin' Good Friday No' Bad Friday?"

"I send to you my Valentine
Wi' bleedin' hearts galore,
I grudged tae buy a bleedin' stamp
So I stuck it through the door."

"Ma man wantit mair fibre in his diet so ah gave him a daud o' auld carpet."

"Ma man objects tae nudes that much on the stage he goes every night tae boo them."

"Ah want tae know the official startin' an' finishin' dates for the season o' Peace and Goodwill."

"Remember when we're showin' the gemme tae them next door it's ca'd Back Gammon no' Biled Ham."

"He packed in eatin' eggs as soon as he heard ye could go tae work on wan!"

"Ah seem tae remember me an' you drawin' up a social contract thirty year ago an' IT husnae been a howling success."

THE LAW

The law is of course an ass, and an ass is quite useful if you fancy a lift. This ass goes in for lifting people.

Come on, let us not be frivolous about Britain's finest. It's nice to see them out there, ready to pounce on evil and keep life nice for us innocent creatures who need protecting from all kinds of things I have no intention of listing.

I have no intention of lifting either. Like Stephen Leacock, I had Presbyterian ancestors from whom I inherited my staunch and rugged fear of the police.

The great thing about the law, of course, is that it can look absolutely dandy on the statute books, and unbelievably boring as well, but when it slides out from there into daily life, it is operated by a very odd, unpredictable race of creatures called people. And the great basic talent of that race is in getting things wrong and creating confusion.

Judges, of course, know everything, which is why it's often totally impossible to understand a word they say.

The cop on the beat is a much more human and comprehensible animal, even if often his beat is a stretch of road to be whizzed along at high speed just before you leap out to flag him down to tell him the entire district has been pillaged by creatures with wee green skulls.

He is one of Us. That's probably why many Glaswegians, if a polis glances at them, have a sudden violent desire to vanish up a close in case they start blurting out that they once nicked a buttermilk dainty from Mrs McCafferty's sweetie shop when they were under the influence of a sweet tooth. What they are realising unconsciously is that the cop himself once did the same thing when he was six, so he has an X-ray vision of the sheer evil of the human animal from experience.

True story from away back. A jokester sent telegrams to six friends, reading FLEE THE COUNTRY. ALL IS DISCOVERED — A FRIEND. Five of them fled the country. Were they secret pilferers of buttermilk dainties?

So our relationship with the law is a very contradictory affair, and Sigmund Freud could certainly have said something very boring about it. The more important thing is that it's quite fun, as well.

**"Two toilet rolls, three beer cans, four big polismen an'
we're up here in BA-ARLINEE —"**

"There's nae justice.... Jim Watt gets the freedom o' the city
fur thumpin' guys an' ah get sixty days."

"Ah reckon oor Darren's the number wan seed in this court, dae you no' Toammy?"

"Send wan o' yer polis doon tae the infirmary tae chairge ma man wi' wife batterin' as soon as he regains consciousness."

"There must be a better way o' protestin' than takin' slates aff the roof."

"I would remind the accused that he is not helping his case by answering 'Pass' to every question."

"Ah can only put it doon tae metal fatigue."

"For the next six months you'll HAVE a fixed address."

"Ah washed mine last night an' ah canny do a thing with it!"

"That makes it easy, Sergeant, we'll jist look for somebo
that's clean shaven."

"Right, Jimmy, youse walk oot an' we'll walk oot in sympathy."

"Ye can arrest me, son, if ye think it'll help yer chances."

"In case ye wiz wunderin', ah'm anither yin that husnae been wi' a call girl in London's west end."

"Ye go oot for an hour's exercise an' whit dae ye get? Squatters!"

"An' tae think ah should be at that dinner-dance the night wearin' the mink stole ah stole."

"The jury have been unable to agree on a verdict."

"Ah suppose they've got tae start their public spending cuts somewhere."

"Naw, it's no' Nigel Mansell, he jist thinks he's Nigel Mansell."

"Ah'm no' comin' fae a party, ah'm jist goin' tae a party."

"Ah didnae think acceptin' a free bell wi' ma new bike wid make me a bent polis."

Dampt disgrace! Ah reckon thae prisoners should get the jile."

"Plain clothes duty disnae necessarily mean the Miss Marple look, W.P.C."

"That's ridic'lous when ye're only up fur parkin' on a yellow line."

"See whit happens when the civil servants don't send ye yer provisional licence!"

WEANS

The wee angels. Really, there is something about a young child, the innocence, the enthusiasm, the vulnerability, that brings a rush of mushy sentiments to our heads. We respond by checking our wallets and bullet-proof vests and get close to a convenient wall.

The reassuring thing is that there is no such thing as a typical wean. A kid can be soft as butter, hard as granite, bright as a button, thick as two short planks, honest as a long day, working out a bank robbery. And that's just one kid I'm talking about.

And they get into trouble. They defy parental orders. As a wean I was ordered not to climb dykes. I clumb dykes. There was one I got on to in the back court and couldn't get down because it was too high to jump. I started to dreep, looking down and knew I would break both legs. Couldn't climb back up again. So I just jung and screamed till an older sister heard the familiar brat voice and came down and across the back court to prise me off.

I was actually a very nice wee boy (he blustered). But I did get led astray by older delinquents and hung on the back of a lorry. They knew to wait for the next corner and let go when it slowed. I couldn't wait. I let go, went flying and gouged out a groove on the tarmac with my face.

This kind of nonsense is baffling to parents. They have explained the perils, they have shaken their fists, and the wee swine will not take a telling. The adults know all about it because they were daft weans, and they want to pass on their experience as a warning. But if weans learned from their parents' experiences, there would be no such thing as childhood. When the brats grow up and have brats, they will repeat the same sage advice and utter the same powerful threats. They will get nowhere.

The reason is that they have forgotten by now what it is like to be a wean. Those infant experiences trickle down a hole in the memory.

In recent years there has been talk of the generation gap, the mutual lack of understanding between adults and the young. There was none in my young day. We understood each other perfectly well, and hated each other. It was a form of warfare. We kicked adults' doors, we terrified old women to death with the evil activity of clockwork, we walked on the grass in the park not because we fancied it, but to assert our savagery against adult bans. It was rare. We stuffed up the wash-house chimneys in order to fill the places with smoke and make life sheer hell for the poor wummin boiling her clothes below. We tied door handles together and then rang both bells. We stole hurls on trams. We put halfpennies on the rails to have them squashed out into pennies. The fact that it didn't work was irrelevant. Adults chased us and cuffed us. They didn't cure us, they merely inflamed us.

Pure murder for adults, of course, because deep down they know that kids are incurable – kids today, that is. They were angels, and they're good at suppressing the memories of their lives of crime.

Unfortunately, kids are actually curable, in the sense that with any luck they'll live long enough to stop being kids and turn into adults with suppressed memories. In the meantime, the war goes on, the total incomprehension goes on, and life would be a lot drearier without it.

"Now, remember — You be back here by three o'clock in the mornin'."

"Remember tae fold yer crisp bag up neatly before ye
throw it doon on the pavement, son."

"Education disruptit again ... Nae wonder hauf the graffiti on the walls is spelt wrang."

"Ye never see yer mother goin' oot wi' a skirt like that."

"And how are we coping since we stopped using the belt,
Mr Carruthers?"

"Too bad that some o' youse is no' goin' for tae get as good
an education as whit some o' us yins got."

"Ye realise, of course, that this is a typical Tory ploy tae keep us aff the unemployed register."

"Ah widnae huv Prince Andrew in a gift, wid you, Irene?"

"Haw, Andra, ye're never gonny believe whit they want fur their Christmases — he wants a necklace an' she wants a bunnet."

"In ma day there wis nae permissive society, jist the Co-operative Society, but it paid dividends!"

"We wid be able tae claim extra money fur unsocial hours."

"There's a barra supplied wi' this model tae save ye humphin' it when ye're oot annoyin' people."

"They will be worn for teaching up to 11 year olds ... For over 11 year olds riot shields will be issued."

"Sandra! Ye're drop oot's dropped in."

"Here ye are, son, pent yer fingers green an' away doon tae the Garden Festival an' ask fur a joab."

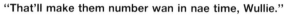

"That'll make them number wan in nae time, Wullie."

"Each of you will write one hundred times 'My teacher is grossly underpaid'."

"It's either a boy goin' tae play a guitar or a lassie goin' tae play tennis."

"Haw Debbie Jane, here's wan wi' a face like Prince Charles wantin' a Princess Di herr cut."

"Is that the loodest station ye can get, Kevin?"

"Ye can get that thing converted tae paraffin for a kick-off."

"Ah had nae sex education at school an' ah've got oan fine."

"That could be very embarrassing!"

"Something lookin' fur ye, Gloria."

"Now remember, shove yersel' in front o' everybody else, wave yer flag then gie her the flooers an' curtsey an' if ye don't dae it right there's a leatherin' when ye get hame."

"If they're a' that clever why are they still just students, Agnes?"

"Or Kevin fancied bein' a politician but they said he wisnae a big enough blether."

"Ah usually stay in at night an' watch television."

"ist imagine, Wullie. Skip twa dinners an' we'll huv the price o' a' packet o' fags!"

"Ah let them watch sex, crime an' violence but ah switch aff the news."

"We had tae stoap ... wur trany packed in."

"In ma day it wis weans that went absent."

"Has it ever occurred tae you that if somebody hadnae inventit denim hauf the population wid be walkin' aboot in their shirt tail!"

"He looks bad enough in this country, goodness knows whit he'll look like upside-doon!"

HEALTH

It is well known, from many surveys and polls and so on, that the Scots are quite sick. They drink more than their English neighbours, possibly because they tend to buy rounds oftener, while the English cuddle a half-pint and make sure they are never on the bell.

Other surveys tell different stories, because the people who make a living out of surveys have to keep going on and on about it, in the hope of getting their numbers in the papers. We are not actually obsessed with health, we just think about it a lot, and look at the neighbours a lot, and realise they are not playing the game.

Well, smoking, for heaven's sake. We look at neighbours who don't merely smoke, they burst into flames. And we are bothered about them, while we squirt water into our own ears, just in case.

People who live in the West of Scotland tend to cough a lot. But maybe that is because they are trying to get into the conversation, and the cough is the intro to an important statement, like, "Isn't it your turn for a round?" A discreet cough, a mere interruption of the chat, could be diagnosed by some medico as a chest condition, when it is merely a scream for help.

We tend, in this part of the world, to be a wee bit fatalist. I have a friend, approaching 90, who has been exhorted by his doctors to chuck the fags because nicotine may shorten his life. The doctor is right, of course. Doctors are always right. If he goes on dragging at the fags, he may not make 200.

There were these two irreligious looking blokes passing a Wayside Pulpit which proclaimed "Bring your doubts to Jesus". And one said to the other, "I never knew he smoked."

Oh, the fags will destroy us, whatever meaning you attach to the word fag. When the world realised that the terrible tobacco weed was actually quite a nasty threat, the doctors were quite right to condemn it. It was a Glasgwegian who got bothered about the implications of their warnings. They seemed to say that if you smoke, you will die; if you don't, you won't. This stubborn keelie, who quite liked a drag, looked into the statistics. He found that very few non-smokers born in the 19th century were still about the place. When he checked on the non-smokers of the 18th century, it was a total wipe-out. These people had done their best, but they sort of croaked, regardless.

So it may be that the Lowland Scot has a sceptical view of what doctors tell him, if he happens to be listening at the time. Maybe he is dedicated to the idea that you live and you die, and there are times when he isn't too sure which of these things he is doing. If he has been doing his reading, he knows that Robert the Bruce was a leper, so maybe leprosy is quite upmarket, and if you suddenly turn up at the Barras with funny marks on your face the populace will slap a crown on your head, or a pint mug, or anything else available.

I have a distant relative who enjoys poor health. I mean, she really enjoys it. Nobody else does, but it is her hobby, it is her importance. You have to be nice to her all the time because she's got This Thing. Oh, what fun that is for her. Other relatives do tend to emigrate, of course, to Beirut or anywhere, because they don't really appreciate her qualifications for stardom. But she will always find another eejit who can pour out sympathy, and bile, on hearing about the wummin's constant suffering. She has spent the last 30 years having the time of her death.

Whether you realise it or not, I take this whole thing very seriously. Health is quite important, I tend to think. And something like dying is not all that funny, unless you like sick jokes. My friends, the sick joke is the only defence we have against our mortality. If we cannot laugh about health, we will die. Aye, that'll be right.

If we *can* laugh about health, we might die. Die laughing, and that's not too terrible. In this part of the world we know that life is real, life is earnest, and the gravy is the goal. The grave can wait till efter. Let's get stuck in at the gravy in the meantime, and have a lot of fun swapping symptoms.

Suddenly I've got this twinge. I think it's an incurable ailment of the humerus, or the funny-bone. Hypochondria can be fun. Read on.

"D'you ever wonder, nurse, what doctors told patients
before the virus was invented?"

"Collected a fortune.... wis sponsored fur fifty pee a blister."

"You've got a top ten there that would even baffle description by Jimmy Saville!"

"Because o' Health Service cuts ye'll need tae get aff an' shove."

"That's ridiculous, whit dae they think we pay wur National Health stamps fur!"

"After six months, we seem to have cracked it, Mr Wilson, you're allergic to grapes."

"Ah fell an' broke ma leg comin' oot a health food shop."

"The National Health Service seems tae be in a terrible state, Mrs McCallum."

"Lucky old you bein' on the waitin' list, ah'm waitin' tae go on the list that's waitin' tae go on the waitin' list."

"We seem tae be the lucky wans."

"Ah love health food but it gives me indigestion."

"Ah hope they're no' referrin' tae us, Brian."

"Well, at least, they canny blame me an' you, Mrs Wilson.
We've gave them wur regular custom."

"Ah keep gettin' this nightmare that ah'm married tae Edwina Currie an' Mrs Thatcher's ma mother-in-law."

"Funny, i'ntit', oot here we're ancillary workers, in there we're skivvies."

"Ah'm workin' ma way up tae bein' a brain surgeon."

"It wis love at first sight, but that wis before National Health specs."

"Ah tell ye whit, Jimmy, you get me ma passport an' ah'll gie ye a hurl in ma ambulance."

"Typical, i'ntit, up go the prescription charges jist before the post-Budget depression epidemic sets in."

"It'll be ma turn next, ah'd better make up ma mind whit's wrang wi' me."

"He says ah've got a tennis elbow an' here's me husnae played tennis fur over a fortnight."

"Ah wid hate tae live in a' that L.A. smog, wid you no', Andra?"

"O.K., last Wednesday wis the day tae stop smokin' so ah stopped smokin' last Wednesday."

"Ah went tae jine a slimmin' club but ah got stuck in the door."

"Your report has come back, Mrs McCallum, and the news is good... it seems you're only a raging hypochondriac."

"Actually, you've got hay fever, so my advice would be to keep well away from hay."

"Dae ah take the valium before or efter ah read ma rates notice, doctor?"

"See smokin'.... ye've nae sooner started efter stoapin' than ye've got tae begin stoapin' again."

"The health warnin' oan thur packets is nae use, ah'm coughin' as bad as ever!"